Quilts from Squier Lane

by Diane Albeck-Grick

Enjoy Mary!

Diane Albeck-Grick

Chitra Publications

Montrose, Pennsylvania

Your Best Value in Quilting
www.QuiltTownUSA.com

Welcome to

The Horse Barn

The Granary

The Farmhouse

Just three miles outside the small town of Nicholson in rural Wyoming County, Pennsylvania, our family farm sits at the end of a dirt road called Squier Lane. Nestled in the heart of the Endless Mountains, the farm experienced five generations working its soil to help provide for their families. Much has changed since the farm was settled in the mid 1850s. However, one thing remained constant throughout five generations—the family's love of quilting.

My fondest childhood memories include visiting Grandpa Squier's farm nearly every weekend. It was always fun and magical. I spent many happy hours swinging on the tire that hung from the old spruce tree, running through hayfields with Grandpa's beagle, and riding in the bucket of Grandpa's Allis Chalmers tractor.

Grandpa Squier

When the cold weather set in, I retreated to the inside of the family homestead and was warmed by the heat of the woodstove in the kitchen. During the long winter months when the cold wind blew, I would go on "adventures" in the house. There, my love for antiques began.

The bedrooms upstairs were my favorite places to explore. Within those old lathe and plaster walls, I would find old clothes and shoes to play dress-up, old baby dolls to care for and worn-out quilts to wrap them in.

The Icehouse

The Cow Barn

Adelia Bacon Squier

Mattie's mother-in-law

my Great Grandma

Mattie Miller Squier

Prudence's mother

my Great Aunt

Prudence Squier Walker

Jerry's mother

my Cousin

Jerry R. Walker

Prudence's son

Diane Albeck-Grick

As I entered adulthood, I never tired of my adventures at Grandpa's, especially when I became a fifth generation quilter. It was on one such adventure that I discovered three unfinished quilt tops that were carefully folded up and stored in an old hand-hewn wooden trunk. That was just the beginning.

After Grandpa's death in 1998, we started cleaning out the house, uncovering boxes and opening every dresser drawer. More quilts and fabric came to light. Colorful feedsacks were discovered as well as fabric scraps that belonged to my great-grandma and were found rolled up in a feedbag in a dark closet. I took these treasured scraps home and started sewing. The rest, as they say, is history.

Grandpa taught me to see beauty in everything–especially in life's simplest pleasures which include the basic utility quilts patterned in this book. They are patterns that a beginner can easily achieve and at the same time offer a "piece-ful" reprieve for the more advanced quilter. Try to abandon all the rules that you've been taught were the only acceptable way. Cut a scrap on the bias. Don't obsess about matching points or perfecting your appliqué and quilting stitches. Quilt for the love of it! Slow down your pace and let your mind wander back to a simpler time when your only worry was whether or not the rope on your tire swing would hold or break. Go grab your scrapbag, pull up a chair, and sit a spell. Together we'll take a "stroll" up Squier Lane.

Diane

It is not how much we have, but how much we enjoy, that makes happiness. —Charles H. Spurgeon

Contents

Acknowledgements

Special thanks to the following for helping me make this book a reality:

Don and Rebekah Lee of Americana Roads Antiques, Springville, PA, for allowing me to photograph my quilts in their quaint and charming antique shop;

Verne and Kim, my friends and the current owners of the farm, for letting me make myself at home there whenever I want;

My wonderful family, especially my husband Alan and my son Colvin who unselfishly gave me the extra time I needed to make "just one more stitch;"

and most importantly, my thanks to God, for His abundant blessings.

This charming quilt was one of three unfinished quilt tops that I found tucked away in Grandpa's farmhouse. Although I don't know who made it, I believe the maker was fairly new to appliqué as Sue's curves appear to have been simplified. During a show and tell session, a viewer said Sue looked like she was wearing a lampshade instead of a sunbonnet! I decided later that she must be Sunbonnet Sue's wild cousin of whom you never hear about because of her unique sense of fashion. Please allow me to introduce you to "Lampshade Lucy"!

Lampshade Lucy

and sleeve on one 11" x 12" muslin rectangle. Appliqué the pieces in the same order.

Quilt Size: 49" x 67"
Block Size: 10" x 11"

Materials

- 20 prints, each at least 7" square
- 20 solids, each at least 9" square
- 3 1/2 yards muslin
- 3/4 yard pink for the binding
- 3 yards backing fabric
- 53" x 71" piece of batting
- Black embroidery floss

Cutting

The appliqué pieces are full size and do not include a turn-under allowance. Make a template for each pattern piece. Trace around the templates on the right side of the fabric and add a 1/8" to 3/16" turn-under allowance when cutting the fabric pieces out. All other dimensions include a 1/4" seam allowance.

For each of 20 blocks:

- Cut 1: dress, print
- Cut 1: hat, solid
- Cut 1: sleeve, same solid
- Cut 1: shoe, same solid

Also:

- Cut 12: 3 1/2" squares, assorted solids
- Cut 20: 11" x 12" rectangles, muslin
- Cut 15: 3 1/2" x 11 1/2" strips, muslin
- Cut 16: 3 1/2" x 10 1/2" strips, muslin
- Cut 7: 2 1/2" x 44" strips, pink, for the binding

Directions

1. Center and pin a shoe, dress, hat,

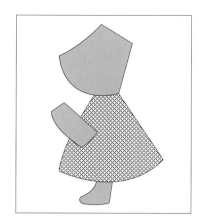

2. Using 2 strands of black embroidery floss, embroider around each appliqué piece with running stitches.

3. Embroider the details on the sleeve and hat in the same manner.

4. Embroider the hand and the ribbon on the muslin background.

Ode to Lampshade Lucy

Lucy was always different, and no one ever knew
that she was a first cousin of sunbonnet-wearing Sue.

Sue was always proper, living strictly by the book.
Lucy liked to be unique, always making others look.

Sue was having a patch party next week, the invite said
and the only things Lucy could "sew" were weeds in her flower bed.

The day of the party came and Lucy was filled with dread.
She didn't own a single needle or spool of sewing thread.

The other gals might frown on the sewing skills she lacked,
so she planned to give them something else to talk about
behind her back.

Everyone would have sunbonnets to perch upon their heads.
She knew that she was different, so she'd wear a lampshade instead!

When Lucy arrived at the party, they couldn't believe their eyes.
To see Lucy wearing a lampshade was quite a big surprise.

The room grew very quiet, as no one was prepared to see a lampshade
on Lucy's head, so they dropped their needles and stared.

Then the group began to laugh, and that just goes to show that
being unique is quite all right, whether or not you can sew!

— Diane Albeck-Grick

5. Using 3 strands of black floss, embroider 3 French knots on the shoe to complete the block. Make 20.

6. Trim each block to 10 1/2" x 11 1/2", keeping the design centered.

Assembly

1. Lay out the blocks in 5 rows of 4, placing the 3 1/2" x 11 1/2" strips vertically between the blocks. Lay out the 3 1/2" x 10 1/2" muslin strips horizontally between the blocks, placing the 3 1/2" solid squares between the horizontal muslin strips.

2. Sew the blocks, squares, and strips into horizontal rows.

3. Join the rows.

4. Finish the quilt as described in the *General Directions*, using the 2 1/2" x 44" pink strips for the binding.

French Knot

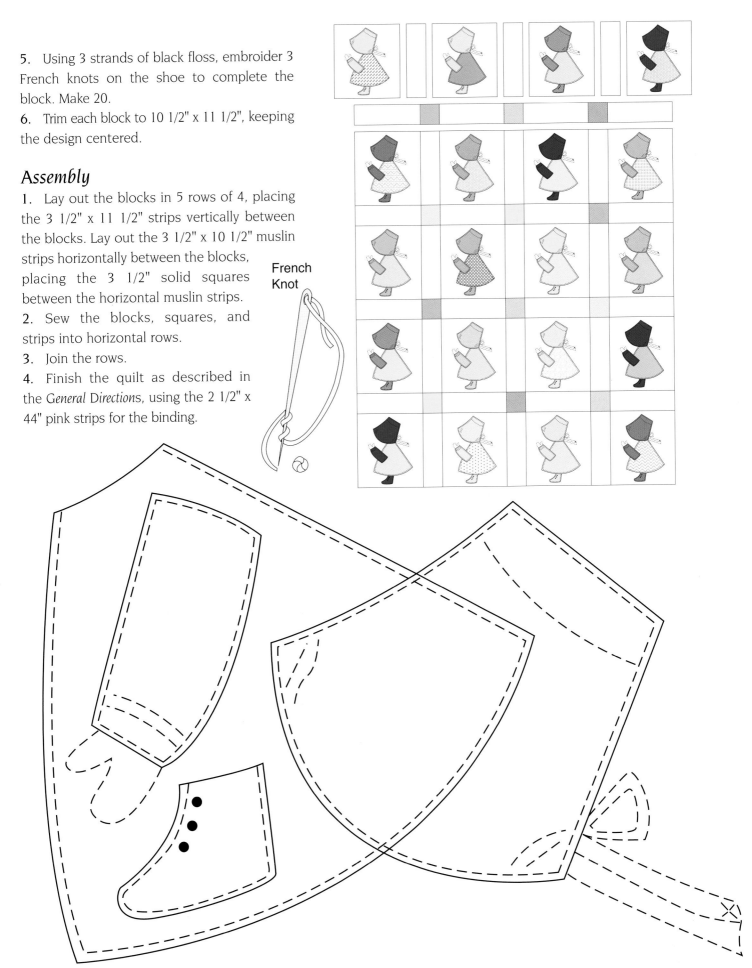

Album Quilt

Quilt Size: 75 1/2" x 79 1/2"
Block Size: 11 3/8" square

Materials

- 16 assorted prints, each at least 12" square
- 5 1/2 yards muslin
- 4 1/2 yards backing fabric
- 80" x 84" piece of batting

Cutting

Dimensions include a 1/4" seam allowance.

From each print:

- Cut 4: 2 1/2" x 6 1/2" strips
- Cut 8: 2 1/2" squares

From the muslin:

Cut lengthwise strips before cutting other pieces from the same yardage.

- Cut 2: 8 1/2" x 78" lengthwise strips
- Cut 5: 6 1/2" x 66" lengthwise strips
- Cut 8: 2 1/2" x 44" strips, for the binding
- Cut 16: 2 1/2" x 6 1/2" strips
- Cut 32: 2 1/2" squares
- Cut 48: 4 1/8" squares, then cut them in quarters diagonally to yield 192 side triangles
- Cut 32: 2 3/8" squares, then cut them in half diagonally to yield 64 corner triangles
- Cut 12: 6 1/2" x 11 7/8" strips

Directions

For each block:

1. Stitch two 2 1/2" print squares to opposite sides of a 2 1/2" muslin square to make a pieced strip. Make 2.

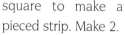

2. Stitch the pieced strips to opposite sides of a 2 1/2" x 6 1/2" muslin strip to make the center section. Set it aside.

3. Stitch 2 side triangles to a 2 1/2" print square. Stitch a corner triangle to the top to make a corner unit, as shown. Make 4.

4. Stitch a corner unit to a 2 1/2" x 6 1/2" print strip. Make 2. Stitch the units to opposite sides of the center section.

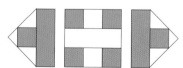

5. Stitch 2 side triangles to a 2 1/2" x 6 1/2" print strip. Make 2.

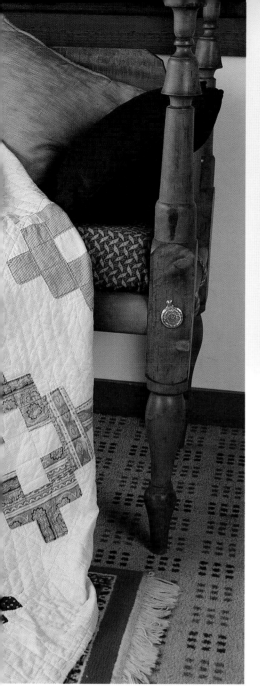

Dreams of Yesterday

Mourning prints, turkey reds,
shades of cadet blue,
squares of tiny shirting prints,
I think there are a few.
These scraps up in the attic lay,
they are dreams of yesterday.

Conversation prints, pastel flowers,
aprons past their prime,
a square of Grandma's Sunday best
in colors softened by time.
These scraps were found in disarray;
they are dreams of yesterday.

Feedbags replaced crisp cotton
before and during the war.
Quilts were among the many things
this humble fabric was used for.
Feedsacks held grain and seeds for hay
that planted dreams of yesterday.

Leftover pieces from home-ec. class
and 4-H projects for the fair,
the fabrics found within these quilts
were chosen with thought and care.
When these pieces start to fray,
they'll still be dreams of yesterday.

— Diane Albeck-Grick

strips between the blocks in the vertical rows. Stitch the blocks and strips into rows, as shown in the Assembly Diagram.

2. Measure the rows. Trim the 6 1/2" x 66" muslin strips to that measurement. Stitch the strips between the rows and to the right and left sides.

3. Measure the width of the quilt. Trim the 8 1/2" x 78" muslin strips to that measurement. Stitch them to the top and bottom of the quilt.

4. Finish the quilt as described in the *General Directions*, using the 2 1/2" x 44" muslin strips for the binding.

6. Stitch a corner unit to each pieced strip. Stitch the units to the remaining sides of the center section to complete a block. Make 16.

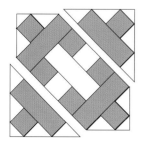

Assembly

1. Lay out the blocks in 4 rows of 4. Place the 6 1/2" x 11 7/8" muslin

rowing up, I spent many Saturdays down at Grandpa Squier's farm. A lot of my time was spent swinging on the tire that hung from the tall spruce tree in the front yard. But once the warm days of June came, it was time to abandon the swing and begin the process of planting the garden.

When I was little, I would be assigned the task of planting rows of green beans or some other vegetable whose seeds did not require delicate handling. Once that was done, I was the delegated water girl who gave all the tomato plant holes a good drink of water before the plants were placed in the freshly dug earth. The days were never quite long enough to finish the entire garden, so my mom and my sister and I would spend the night at Grandpa's and hope the next day's weather would be just as kind. We'd all enjoy a bowl of Neapolitan ice cream while watching Saturday-night television before my sister and I were sent to bed.

After spreading some old quilts out on the hardwood floor for our bedding, we would quietly make up stories about what ghost might be living in the attic. Eventually we'd drift off to sleep to the lullaby of crickets and tree toads humming in the warm summer night air. There was a double bed in the bedroom, but only Mom had the privilege of sleeping in it. That wasn't because she was older than us, but to avoid the squabble that would inevitably occur while trying to remember who slept there last time.

After being awakened at the crack of dawn by the neighbors' crowing roosters, I'd hurry downstairs so I could enjoy the quietness of the morning. As I'd sit at the dining-room table eating a bowl of corn flakes, the rising sun would begin burning off the fog that lingered over the meadow. There was nothing like the feeling of walking barefoot in the dewy morning grass and listening to the "galump" of the frogs waking up in the pond. Another beautiful day had begun at the farm.

Double T

Quilt Size: 79 3/4" square
Block Size: 8 1/4" square

Materials
- 6 1/2 yards blue
- 2 1/2 yards muslin
- 5 yards backing fabric
- 84" square of batting

Cutting
Dimensions include a 1/4" seam allowance.

From the blue fabric:
- Cut 8: 3 1/4" x 76" strips
- Cut 2: 3 1/4" x 81" strips
- Cut 9: 2 1/2" x 44" strips, for the binding
- Cut 42: 3 1/4" x 8 3/4" strips
- Cut 196: 2 1/2" x 4" rectangles
- Cut 98: 4" squares, then cut them in quarters diagonally to yield 392 triangles

From the muslin:
- Cut 49: 2 1/2" squares
- Cut 98: 4" squares, then cut them in quarters diagonally to yield 392 small triangles
- Cut 98: 3 5/8" squares, then cut them in half diagonally to yield 196 large triangles

Directions
1. Stitch two 2 1/2" x 4" blue rectangles to opposite sides of a 2 1/2" muslin square.

2. Stitch 2 small muslin triangles to opposite sides of a 2 1/2" x 4" blue rectangle, as shown. Make 2.

3. Stitch the 2 pieced units to opposite sides of the pieced strip. Trim the blue rectangles even with the muslin triangles, as shown.

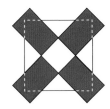

4. Stitch 2 blue triangles to a small muslin triangle to make a side unit, as shown. Make 4.

5. Stitch the side units to the block center. Stitch 4 large muslin triangles to the corners to complete a block. Make 49.

Assembly
1. Referring to the photo, stitch 7 blocks and six 3 1/4" x 8 3/4" blue strips together alternately to make a row. Make 7.

2. Measure the block rows. Trim the 3 1/4" x 76" blue strips to that measurement.

3. Stitch the trimmed sashing strips between the rows and to the top and bottom.

4. Measure the length of the quilt. Trim the 3 1/4" x 81" blue strips to that measurement and stitch them to the sides of the quilt.

5. Finish the quilt as described in the *General Directions*, using the 2 1/2" x 44" blue strips for the binding.

essert was something we could always count on at Grandpa's house as long as somebody else brought it. That was because Grandpa was a farmer, not a baker. Brownies and ice cream, blueberry pudding or fresh homemade applesauce served over biscuits were perennial favorites in our family.

But there was one dessert I knew I could count on every February. Grandpa and I shared birthdays, his being February 14 and mine falling on the 12th. His favorite dessert, second only to apple pie, was chocolate cake with peanut butter icing. Birthdays were never a big gala affair but celebrated rather informally at his farm with immediate family present. Sharing birthdays was fun except that Grandpa always got a bigger piece of cake than I did!

Having grown up on the farm and being a retired farmer, Grandpa learned the value of being thrifty—a trait that rubbed off on me. Because of this, he enjoyed woodworking and often made some small gift to give to me for my birthday. He made a small pine jewelry box for me in 1976. The last thing he ever made was my three-rail quilting frame, one of my most cherished possessions. I learned at a very young age that "presence" is much more important than presents, and that time spent with family can never be bought in a store. I know this to be true as birthdays haven't been the same since Grandpa passed away in May 1998. There will always be an empty dessert plate in my heart, but fortunately memories, like chocolate cake with peanut butter icing, are sweet—and sometimes sweeter.

Dessert Plate

Quilt Size: 58" x 72 1/2"
Block Size: 14 1/2" square

Materials

- Assorted scraps at least 3" x 5" and totaling 4 1/2 yards
- 1/3 yard yellow print
- 4 1/2 yards muslin
- 5/8 yard fabric for the binding
- 3 1/2 yards backing fabric
- 62" x 77" piece of batting

Cutting

Pattern pieces (on page 31) are full size and include a 1/4" seam allowance, as do all dimensions given.

For each of 20 blocks:

- Cut 20: A, assorted prints

Also:

- Cut 20: B, yellow print
- Cut 20: 15 1/2" squares, muslin
- Cut 7: 2 1/2" x 44" strips, binding fabric

Directions

For each block:

1. Stitch 2 A's together in a pair. Start stitching at the narrow end. Stop 1/4" from the wide end and backstitch. Make 10.

2. Stitch 5 pairs together to make a half plate. Make 2.

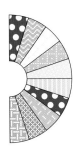

3. Stitch 2 half plates together to make a plate. Make 20.

4. Press the outside edge of a plate under 1/4". Center and pin the plate on a 15 1/2" muslin square.

5. Appliqué the plate on the muslin square.

6. Press the edge of a yellow print B under 1/4". Trim the seam allowance to 1/8" to reduce bulk, if necessary.

7. Pin the B to the plate, covering the seam allowance of the center of the plate.

8. Appliqué the B to the plate to complete a block. Make 20.

9. Trim the blocks to 15" square.

Assembly

1. Lay out the blocks in 5 rows of 4.

2. Stitch the blocks into rows. Join the rows.

3. Finish the quilt as described in the *General Directions* using the 2 1/2" x 44" strips for the binding.

Full-Size Patterns are on page 31

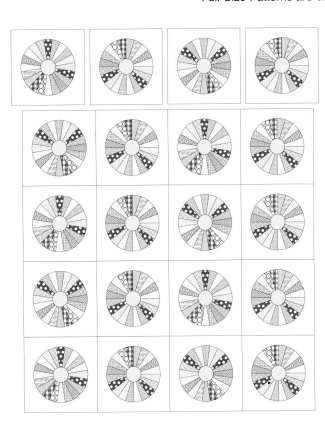

Grandpa Squier's dining room was the most important room in the farmhouse. It was a place where my whole family would sit down together at the old oak table and enjoy good food and each others' company—well, most of the time. Occasionally, my sister and I would argue over who would get to sit in the "sacred" chair next to Grandpa. This dispute was always solved quickly as Grandpa, in his infinite wisdom, would bring to our attention that he had a right and a left side so we could both sit next to him. After we cleaned our plates, Grandpa often would lean back in his plank-bottom chair and tell stories. Some we had heard before, but we never tired of hearing them again. One in particular was about my great-great-great-grandpa William

Miller, who in the 1850s emigrated from Germany and settled on 92 acres where the farm still stands. I often wondered why he came clear across the ocean, halfway around the world to settle here in the heart of the rolling Endless Mountains. Working the land with such primitive equipment available in the 1850s couldn't have been easy, especially since very little of the land on the farm is flat and much of it is rock laden. Never knowing him, I feel the farm is a testament to his determined and hard-working character that I admired so much in my Grandpa. I like to think that maybe the beauty of Pennsylvania's mountains captured his soul and that maybe he felt as I do now—no matter where I travel, there will never be a place as special as the farm that sits at the end of Squier Lane.

Postcards from the Past

Quilt Size: 73 1/2" x 82 1/2"
Block Size: 2 3/4" x 5 1/4"

Materials

- 420 assorted prints, each at least 3 1/4" x 5 3/4", half light and half dark in reds, blues, tans, browns, and blacks for a total of 6 yards
- 3/4 yard red print for the binding
- 78" x 87" piece of backing fabric
- 78" x 87" piece of batting

Cutting

Dimensions include a 1/4" seam allowance.

- Cut 210: 3 1/4" x 5 3/4" rectangles, light prints
- Cut 210: 3 1/4" x 5 3/4" rectangles, dark prints
- Cut 8: 2 1/2" x 44" strips, red print, for the binding

Directions

1. Lay out the 3 1/4" x 5 3/4" rectangles in 30 rows of 14, alternating light and dark prints.
2. Stitch the rectangles into rows.
3. Join the rows.
4. Finish the quilt as described in the General Directions using the 2 1/2" x 44" red print strips for the binding.

The Patch-work Quilt

by Eve Egleston Hoyt
Published in *Farm and Home*, March 1921 or 1924

One day while treasure hunting in the farmhouse, I discovered a box containing many quilt columns that had been clipped and saved from various newspapers. Among them, I found this lovely poem which originally appeared in a 1920s edition of *Farm and Home*, a magazine for rural folk, published until 1945.

The white dress she was married in,
The onyx earrings and the pin
Of coral, and the chain of gold,
The point-lace kerchief, rare and old,
The robin's-egg-blue silk, her rings
Her satin slippers, tiny things:
Daguerreotype and cameo,
Are treasured keep-sakes now, but oh

Of all the treasures I can boast
I love the patch-work quilt the most.
She pieced it in the long ago,
With patient stitches, fine and slow,
Each block devised of dark and light
Small diamond pieces, looking quite
Like piled-up boxes, or like stairs
To lead you upwards unawares.

Even today I know so well
The little story she would tell
About each piece; "That pink and white
Batiste was auntie's, and the bright
Red cashmere was a dress of mine
When I was only eight or nine.
That piece was grandpa's dressing gown,
My polonaise was that dark brown.

That little gingham check was yours,
That white piece was your pinafores.
Your best sunbonnets were that blue,
A lovely chambric, ruffled too,
And stiffly starched; that turkey red
Your little aprons when your head
Scarce reached my waist; this pink and brown
Was your small Mother Hubbard gown.

That dark blue challie with the spray
Of yellow roses had a train,
And Watteau plaits; this apple-green
Moire was mine; the brown sateen
Was auntie's basque, and all the black
That forms the edges and the back
Was grandma's gown of silk brocade,
She gave me when the quilt was made."

I almost hear her voice once more,
And see the quaint old things she wore,
The dolman, and the Paisley shawl,
My self a child again, and all
My childish faith and love surge up
To fill my worn heart's empty cup:
Of all the things she once possessed,
I love the patch-work quilt the best.

During the winter, Grandpa always had one of his homemade bird feeders hanging from the spruce tree in the front yard. "What kind of bird is that?" was one of the many questions I asked Grandpa as we sat by the window in the dining room. I knew I could count on him to know the answer without looking in the bird reference book which was always kept in the Larkin desk that sat in the living room. The snowy ground became alive with color as the cardinals, blue jays, and chickadees ate their fill. I began to recognize the different birds as well as their unique sounds–especially the doves as they called to each other, roosting safely in the distant evergreens.

In the late spring, it was always fun to watch the robins pull worms after the garden had been plowed for the first time. In the warmth of summer, I took delight in watching the barn swallows build their nests and raise their young. When the cool autumn days approached, I watched with wonder as the geese assembled in a "V" formation to make the trip south before the cold winter made its return.

In 1994, Grandpa made a bird feeder and gave it to my husband and me as a wedding present. As I sit and quilt in our living room next to the deck, I love watching the birds and occasional squirrel stop to dine on sunflower seeds. I've come to realize that this homemade feeder not only feeds wildlife, but also my memories.

Dove in the Window

Quilt Size: 78 1/2" x 87 1/2"
Block Size: 8 3/4" square

Materials

- 1/2 yard each of 9 assorted prints
- 6 yards muslin
- 5 1/4 yards backing fabric
- 83" x 92" piece of batting

Cutting

Dimensions include a 1/4" seam allowance.

From each print:

- Cut 10: 2 1/4" squares
- Cut 5: 6 1/8" squares, then cut them in half diagonally to yield 10 triangles
- Cut 8: 5 1/4" squares

From the muslin:

- Cut 9: 2 1/2" x 44" strips, for the binding
- Cut 45: 9 5/8" squares, then cut them in half diagonally to yield 90 large triangles
- Cut 90: 2 5/8" squares, then cut them in half diagonally to yield 180 small triangles
- Cut 72: 5 1/4" squares

Directions

1. Draw diagonal lines from corner to corner on the wrong side of each 5 1/4" muslin square. Draw horizontal and vertical lines through the centers.

2. Place a marked muslin square on a 5 1/4" print square, right sides together.

Sew 1/4" away from the diagonal lines on both sides. Make 8 using matching 5 1/4" print squares.

3. Cut the squares on the drawn lines to yield 64 pieced squares. You will use 60. Press the seam allowances toward the print.

4. Lay out 3 pieced squares and a small muslin triangle and sew them into a row, as shown. Make 10.

5. Lay out 3 pieced squares, a 2 1/4" print square, and a small muslin triangle and sew them into a row, as shown. Make 10.

6. Sew a short row to a print triangle. Sew a long row to the triangle.

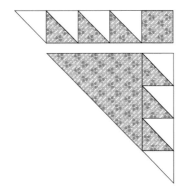

7. Sew a large muslin triangle to the pieced unit to complete a block. Make 10.

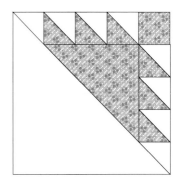

8. Make 10 blocks from each of the remaining prints for a total of 90 blocks.

Assembly

1. Lay out the blocks in 10 rows of 9. Sew the blocks into rows and join the rows.

2. Finish the quilt as described in the *General Directions*, using the 2 1/2" x 44" muslin strips for the binding.

The last quilt I rescued from Grandpa's farmhouse was this Ohio Star which was found folded up in the back of a closet. Long before I knew of its existence, the quilt had been damaged beyond repair. Water marks are present as well as several holes created by hungry mice. I was inspired to take it home and stitch "Ohio Star Crib Quilt," a close replica using reproduction fabrics which I carefully matched to each block of the original quilt.

Ohio Star

Quilt Size: 69" x 82"
Block Size: 9" square

Materials

- 30 assorted light prints, each at least 9" square
- 30 assorted dark prints, each at least 15" square
- 2 3/4 yards border print
- 2/3 yard brown print for the binding
- 5 yards backing fabric
- 73" x 86" piece of batting

Cutting

Cut the lengthwise strips before cutting other pieces from the same yardage.

For each of 30 blocks:

- Cut 1: 3 1/2" square, light print
- Cut 2: 4 1/4" squares, same light print
- Cut 2: 4 1/4" squares, dark print
- Cut 4: 3 1/2" squares, same dark print

Also:

- Cut 8: 4 1/2" x 76" lengthwise strips, border print

- Cut 25: 4 1/2" x 9 1/2" lengthwise strips, border print
- Cut 8: 2 1/2" x 44" strips, brown print, for the binding

Preparation

1. Draw diagonal lines from corner to corner on the wrong side of each 4 1/4" light print square.

Directions

NOTE: *You may wish to mix some of the pieces to give the block a more scrappy look.*

For each block:

1. Place a marked light print square on a 4 1/4" dark print square, right sides together. Sew 1/4" away from both sides of one diagonal line, as shown. Make 2.

2. Cut the squares on the drawn lines to yield 8 pieced triangles. Press the seam allowances toward the dark print.

3. Sew 2 pieced triangles together to make a pieced square, as shown. Make 4.

4. Lay out the pieced squares, the matching 3 1/2" light print square, and the matching 3 1/2" dark print squares in 3 rows of 3, as shown.

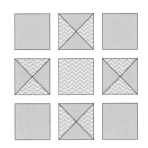

5. Sew the squares into rows. Join the rows to complete an Ohio Star block. Make 30.

Assembly

1. Lay out 6 Ohio Star blocks and five 4 1/2" x 9 1/2" border print strips in a vertical row, as shown in the Assembly Diagram.

2. Join the blocks and strips. Make 5.

3. Measure the length of the rows. Trim 6 of the 4 1/2" x 76" border print strips to that measurement.

4. Lay out the 5 rows and the trimmed border print strips.

5. Join the rows and strips.

6. Measure the width of the quilt. Trim the remaining 4 1/2" x 76" border print strips to that measurement and sew them to the top and bottom of the quilt.

7. Finish the quilt as described in the *General Directions*, using the 2 1/2" x 44" brown print strips for the binding.

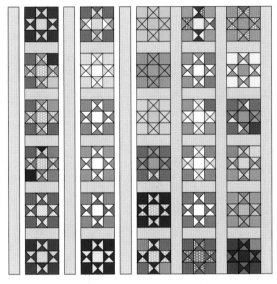

To *make a crib-size* **Ohio Star Quilt**, *use the following* Materials and Cutting lists:

Quilt Size: 42" x 50"
Block Size: 6" square

Materials

- 30 assorted light prints, each at least 6" square
- 30 assorted dark prints, each at least 10" square
- 1 1/2 yards border print
- 1/2 yard brown print for the binding
- 2 1/2 yards backing fabric
- 46" x 54" piece of batting

Cutting

Cut the lengthwise strips before cutting other pieces from the same yardage.

For each of 30 blocks:
- Cut 1: 2 1/2" square, light print
- Cut 2: 3 1/4" squares, same light print
- Cut 2: 3 1/4" squares, dark print
- Cut 4: 2 1/2" squares, same dark print

Also:
- Cut 8: 2 1/2" x 48" lengthwise strips, border print
- Cut 25: 2 1/2" x 6 1/2" lengthwise strips, border print
- Cut 5: 2 1/2" x 44" strips, brown print, for the binding

Harriet Squier-Snell

Leta Squier-Albeck

Mary Jane Squier-Zech

Jn 1939 great-great grandma, Adelia Squier, made a Double Irish Chain crib quilt for Grandma and Grandpa's first born, Aunt Harriet. Great-great-grandma felt that a quilt wasn't truly homemade unless it was stitched entirely by hand, so not surprisingly, this crib quilt was. The "make do with what you have" motto was exhibited by the use of two different greens on the front as well as on the back in which small rectangles of flannel were sewn together using a feather stitch.

Five years later in 1944 it was used for my mom, Leta, and then for the last time in 1951 when my Aunt Mary Jane was born. After a life of frequent washing and patching, it was carefully tucked away until many years later when I discovered I would be having a baby of my own to keep warm.

After Aunt Harriet showed me the fragile remains of the original crib quilt, I decided I would make a replica using the same "make do" motto as great-great-grandma Adelia did in 1939. Instead of buying new fabric to piece the top, I found enough of two different greens tucked away in Grandpa's house to make Colvin's Double Irish Chain. Even though the piecing was done using a machine, the cross-hatch quilting was stitched entirely by hand. Although it isn't homemade according to Adelia's law, I think she would have given her approval just the same.

Irish Chain Crib Quilt

Quilt Size: 40" x 50"
Block Size: 10" square

Materials

- 1 1/2 yards dark green
- 1 1/4 yards bright green
- 1 1/2 yards muslin
- 2 1/2 yards backing fabric
- 44" x 54" piece of batting

Cutting

All dimensions include a 1/4" seam allowance.

From the dark green:

- Cut 4: 6 1/2" x 10 1/2" rectangles
- Cut 1: 6 1/2" x 25" strip
- Cut 5: 2 1/2" x 44" strips, for the binding
- Cut 3: 2 1/2" x 33" strips
- Cut 2: 2 1/2" x 25" strips

From the bright green:

- Cut 6: 6 1/2" x 10 1/2" rectangles
- Cut 1: 6 1/2" x 33" strip
- Cut 2: 2 1/2" x 33" strips
- Cut 6: 2 1/2" x 25" strips

From the muslin:

- Cut 7: 2 1/2" x 33" strips
- Cut 9: 2 1/2" x 25" strips

Directions

For the Block A's:

1. Sew a 6 1/2" x 25" dark green strip between two 2 1/2" x 25" muslin strips to make a panel, as shown. Cut eight 2 1/2" slices from the panel.

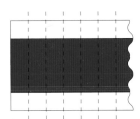

2. Sew a 6 1/2" x 10 1/2" dark green rectangle between two slices to make a dark green Block A, as shown. Make 4.

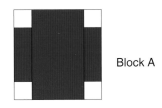

Block A

3. In the same manner, make a panel using the 6 1/2" x 33" bright green strip and the 2 1/2" x 33" muslin strips.

4. Cut twelve 2 1/2" slices from the panel.

5. Sew a 6 1/2" x 10 1/2" bright green rectangle between two slices to make a bright green Block A. Make 6.

For the Block B's:

1. Sew three 2 1/2" x 33" dark green strips and two 2 1/2" x 33" muslin strips together, alternating colors to make a panel, as shown.

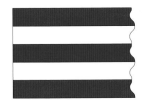

2. Cut twelve 2 1/2" slices from the panel.

3. Sew three 2 1/2" x 25" muslin strips and two 2 1/2" x 25" dark green strips together, alternating colors to make a panel, as shown.

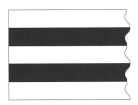

4. Cut eight 2 1/2" slices from the panel.

5. Sew 3 strips from the first group and 2 strips from the second group together along their length, alternating rows to make a dark green Block B, as shown. Make 4.

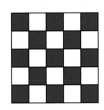

Block B

6. In the same manner, sew three 2 1/2" x 25" bright green strips and the two 2 1/2" x 25" muslin strips together to make a panel. Make 2.

7. Cut eighteen 2 1/2" slices from the panels.

8. Sew three 2 1/2" x 33" muslin strips and the two 2 1/2" x 33" bright green strips together to make a panel.

9. Cut twelve 2 1/2" slices from the panel.

10. Sew 5 slices together along their

(continued on page 23)

Using some of the first vintage fabrics that I discovered hiding in Grandpa's house, I pieced "*Squier Scraps a Tumblin'*." The name is appropriate as the old scraps seemed to keep "tumbling" out from unexpected places. Ninety-five different prints ranging from the 1930s-1960s comprise this charm quilt. The alternate white tumblers were cut from vintage flour sacks. As I sorted through the family scraps, Aunt Harriet and mom took a trip down memory lane, identifying some from childhood clothing, and others from high school home-economic projects. By hand quilting the classic Baptist Fan design, I achieved a traditional, vintage look.

Squier Scraps a Tumblin'

Quilt Size: 37 1/2" x 42 1/2"

Materials

- 95 assorted print scraps, each at least 3 1/2" x 4 1/2"
- 1 1/2 yards muslin
- 1/3 yard blue check
- 1 1/2 yards backing fabric
- 42" x 47" piece of batting

Directions

1. Lay out the tumblers in 10 rows of 19, alternating assorted print tumblers with muslin ones.
2. Sew the tumblers into rows.
3. Join the rows.
4. Trim the short sides of the quilt to straighten the edges.
5. Finish the quilt as described in the *General Directions* using the 2 1/2" x 44" blue check strips for the binding.

Cutting

The tumbler pattern is full size and includes a 1/4" seam allowance, as do all dimensions given.

- Cut 95: tumblers, assorted prints
- Cut 95: tumblers, muslin
- Cut 4: 2 1/2" x 44" strips, blue check, for the binding

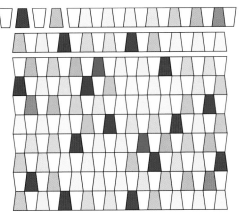

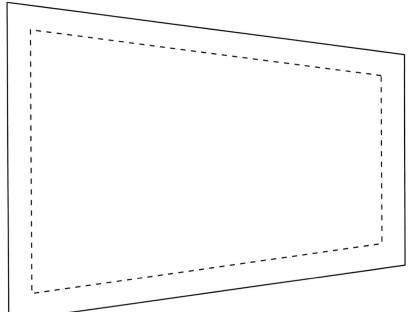

Irish Chain Crib Quilt

(continued from page 21)

length, alternating rows to make a bright green Block B. Make 6.

Assembly

1. Lay out the blocks in 5 rows of 4.

2. Sew the blocks into rows.
3. Join the rows.
4. Finish the quilt as described in the *General Directions* using the 2 1/2" x 44" dark green strips for the binding.

The open areas in this quilt allow for creative quilting. I quilted this design in the lower left dark green Block A. Within the double rectangle I stitched the initials of the quilt recipient, my son, Colvin.

Grandpa always took time to tell me of my ancestors that I didn't have the good fortune of knowing. Most of the people he spoke about had been gone for many years, but Grandpa felt it was important for younger generations to know and be proud of their heritage. Grandpa often talked about his mother, Mattie Miller Squier.

Born in 1881, Great-grandma played many roles throughout her life. She was a school teacher, farmer's wife, and mother to three children. She knew how to play the fiddle and the piano. Being a full-figured woman, Great-grandma was a seamstress out of necessity as well as a quilter. While I do not have any recollections of her, Great-grandma unknowingly left behind her legacy of memories hidden in a scrap bag that I would uncover many years after her death in 1950.

After discovering her scrap bag among many other things that hadn't seen daylight in years, I dumped its contents on the floor. To my delight, I found small bundles of scraps consisting of indigo and cadet blue, gray mourning prints and rich turkey red prints. I knew only one thing could be done with these precious scraps—Make a quilt.

Sitting at my quilt frame carefully making every stitch, I wondered what Great-grandma thought or dreamed about as she stitched her quilts so long ago. I wondered if she quilted after everyone was asleep when the house was quiet. I wondered what her favorite part of making a quilt was. I wondered whether she got knots in her thread like I did or if her heart raced as she put the last stitches in the binding.

I finished "**Mattie's Memory**" shortly before Memorial Day 1997. While visiting her grave I felt a very strong connection—a link that had been made not only through blood, but also through quilting. Memories that are stitched together from one generation to the next can never unravel.

Mattie's Memory

Quilt Size: 72" square
Block Size: 21" square

Materials

- 36 assorted light print scraps (or shirtings), each at least 4 1/2" x 5 1/2"
- 18 assorted red print scraps, each at least 4 1/2" x 5 1/2"
- 90 assorted blue print scraps, each at least 4 1/2" x 5 1/2"
- 3 yards blue print
- 3/4 yard red print for the binding
- 2 yards muslin
- 4 1/2 yards backing fabric
- 76" square of batting

Cutting

The pattern pieces (on page 31) are full size and include a 1/4" seam allowance, as do all dimensions given.

- Cut 36: A, assorted light prints
- Cut 36: A, assorted blue and red prints NOTE: I *used 27 blue print A's and 9 red print A's. Notice there is one red print A in each block center. Use any ratio of blue to red that you like.*
- Cut 72: B, assorted blue and red prints NOTE: I *used one red print B in each of 8 blocks.*
- Cut 12: 4 1/2" x 21 1/2" strips, muslin, for the sashing
- Cut 72: C, muslin
- Cut 9: 21 1/2" squares, blue print
- Cut 4: 4 1/2" squares, blue print
- Cut 9: 2 1/2" x 44" strips, red print, for the binding

Directions

1. Sew a light print A to a blue or red print A to make a pieced unit. Make 36.

2. Join 2 pieced units to make a half-circle. Make 18.

3. Join 2 half-circles to make a block center. Make 9. Set them aside.

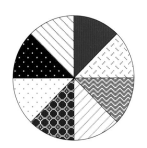

4. Sew a blue or red B to a muslin C to make a pieced unit. Make 72.

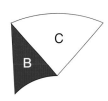

5. Sew 8 pieced units together to make a pieced circle. Make 9.

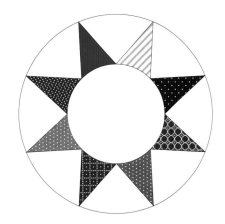

6. Press the edge of each block center under 1/4". Appliqué a block center to a pieced circle, overlapping the circle by 1/4" and matching seamlines to make a star. Make 9.

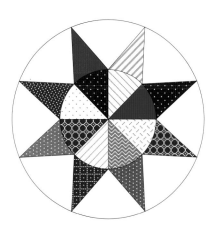

7. Press the outer edge of each star under 1/4". Center and appliqué a star to a 21 1/2" blue print square to complete a Star block. Make 9.

Assembly

1. Lay out three 4 1/2" x 21 1/2" muslin sashing strips and two 4 1/2" blue print squares. Join them to make a sashing row. Make 2.

2. Referring to the quilt photo, lay out the Star blocks, remaining 4 1/2" x 21 1/2" muslin sashing strips and sashing rows.
3. Sew the appliquéd blocks and muslin sashing strips into rows.
4. Join the block rows and sashing rows.
5. Finish the quilt as described in the *General Directions* using the 2 1/2" x 44" red print strips for the binding.

Full-Size Patterns are on page 31

Great-grandma's Sunbonnet Needlecase

Materials

- Fat quarter (18" x 22") fabric for bonnet
- 2 felt scraps, at least 1 1/2" x 2" each
- 2 small snaps
- 2" x 6" piece of cardboard or heavy template material
- Perle cotton or strong hand-quilting thread, to match the fabric

While cleaning out Grandpa's farmhouse, I came across many items that seemed useless but had been saved anyway. Old broken eyeglasses, pocketwatch parts, and empty wooden spools were common finds. I didn't even question myself as to why these things may have been kept. I knew the answer: You might just need 'em some day!

Also I came across an old faded sunbonnet made from blue-and-white checked cotton. It was in bad shape and knowing I couldn't possibly save everything I found, it was thrown out. Some time later among the many scraps of material I discovered, were pieces of dress sleeves in the same blue-and-white checked print as the sunbonnet that had been disposed of earlier. I added the pieces to my vintage fabric collection knowing that someday I'd need it.

While visiting with Great-aunt Prudence a few years later, I enjoyed a show and tell session of the earlier quilts she had made. As I ran my hand over one of the old quilts, I spotted the same blue-and -white checked print that seemed to be following me! After telling her of the sunbonnet and fabric scraps I found at the farm, she stated that her mother, Mattie, had a dress made from that very fabric. I knew right then I'd make a sunbonnet needlecase from the remaining scraps.

The moral of the story is this: Unexpected inspiration can come from trash so if you throw it out, it will likely come back to haunt you!

Cutting

Pattern pieces are on page 32. Dimensions include a 1/4" seam allowance. Transfer all markings after cutting.

- Cut 2: 1" x 15" strips, for the bonnet ties
- Cut 2: bonnets, from fabric
- Cut 4: brims, from fabric (cut 2 with template facing one direction, and 2 facing the reverse)
- Cut 2: brim stays, from cardboard
- Cut 2: 1 1/2" x 2" strips, felt

Directions

1. Stitch 2 brim pieces right sides together as shown. Make 2.

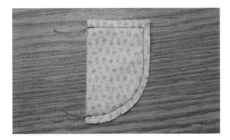

2. Trim the seam allowances to reduce bulk. Turn the brims right side out. Press.
3. Insert the brim stays into the brims.
4. Run a gathering stitch around the rounded side of each bonnet piece between the dots.

5. Baste a felt piece to each brim piece.

6. Pin a brim piece to each side of one bonnet piece at the indicated marks.
7. Pull up the gathering stitches on the bonnet between the markings on each side to fit the brim pieces.

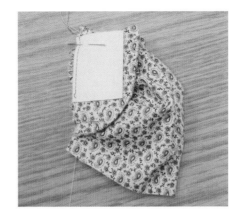

8. Pin to secure the brims in place, then baste the brims to the bonnet.
9. Gather the other bonnet piece around the curved edge to match the measurement of the bonnet piece with the brims.
10. Pin the bonnet pieces right sides together and stitch around the bonnet, leaving the bottom open.
11. Turn the bonnet right side out, pushing the lining into the bonnet.
12. Fold the short end of a 1" x 15" bonnet tie 1/4" toward the wrong side. Finger press. Fold the tie right side in along the length from the folded end to the raw end. Stitch with a scant 1/4" seam allowance. Trim seam allowance to 1/8".

13. Turn the tie right side out. Hand sew the folded end together. Press. Make 2.
14. Press the bottom edge of the bonnet and bonnet lining 1/4" toward the wrong side.
15. Insert the raw edge end of each tie into the bottom of the bonnet, one at each side. Pin in place.

16. Stitch across the bottom of the bonnet close to the edge, securing the ties in the seam at each end.
17. Thread a hand sewing needle with perle cotton or hand quilting thread. Make a knot at the end. Run a gathering stitch about 3/4" above the bottom of the bonnet from side to side. Pull the stitches up to gather the bottom of the bonnet. Knot the thread at the other end.

18. Sew a snap at the top and at the bottom of the brims.
19. Tie scissors to one tie and a spool of thread to the other. HINT: *Stick the end of the tie through the spool center and secure at the other side with a safety pin.*

20. Tuck the thread and scissors into the bonnet and add your thimble. Stick needles and pins into the felt. Snap closed.

Full-Size Patterns are on page 32

Epilogue

The changes of the season were always magnificent at the farm, from the fiery display of the autumn leaves to the individuality of each snowflake during a harsh winter. Knowing that winter couldn't last forever, I always waited impatiently for the first sounds of the peepers to announce that spring was just around the corner. Springtime at Grandpa's farm revealed new life everywhere. Tadpoles swimming in puddles and monarch caterpillars feeding on milkweed were among my favorites.

As a child, Grandpa made me a special wooden box in which to house my newly captured caterpillar friends. It completely amazed me how a wiggly little caterpillar could change into a beautiful butterfly in a relatively short time. After emerging from its cocoon, the time came to let my pretty orange-winged creature go. Setting it free was hard, but I knew it had to be done. I watched it flutter off toward the clouds until it was out of sight. Not until many years later did I understand the life lesson that little caterpillar taught me.

A few years after Grandpa's death, my family was faced with the reality that we could no longer keep the farm and that it had to be sold. No one wanted to see it go but it, too, had to be done. Longtime family friends purchased the farm which helped ease our sadness. Although the farm is no longer ours, the memories will be forever mine and kept safe inside a special wooden box of another sort—my heart.

I still go back to the farm, taking my son Colvin with me. It brings a smile to my face as I watch him run through the fields and explore the barns as I did growing up. Although he is only four-years old, I believe he already treasures great-grandpa's farm and feels it will always be a special place.

As I end this book, I truly hope you enjoyed your visit to Squier Lane. Always remember that some things are meant to be set free, but memories—and quilts—last a lifetime.

At the end of each visit Grandpa always said, "Come again!" We always did, and I hope you will too.

General Directions

ABOUT THE PATTERNS

Read through the pattern directions before cutting fabric. Yardage requirements are based on 44"-wide fabric with a useable width of 42". Pattern directions are given in step-by-step order. If you are sending your quilt to a professional machine quilter, consult them regarding the necessary batting and backing size for your quilt. Batting and backing dimensions listed in the patterns are for hand quilting.

FABRICS

I suggest using 100% cotton. Wash fabric in warm water with mild detergent and no fabric softener. Dry fabric on a warm-to-hot setting. Press with a hot dry iron to remove any wrinkles.

ROTARY CUTTING

Begin by folding the fabric in half, selvage to selvage. Make sure the selvages are even and the folded edge is smooth. Fold the fabric in half again, bringing the fold and the selvages together, again making sure everything is smooth and flat.

Position the folded fabric on a cutting mat so that the fabric extends to the left for right-handed people, or to the right for left-handed people.

With the ruler resting on the fabric, line up the folded edge of the fabric with a horizontal line on the ruler. Trim the uneven edge with a rotary cutter. Make a clean cut through the fabric, beginning in front of the folds and cutting through to the opposite edge with one clean stroke. Always cut away from yourself—never toward yourself!

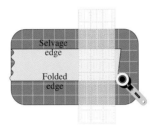

Turn the mat 180°. Move the ruler to the proper width for cutting the first strip and continue cutting until you have the required number of strips. To keep the cut edges even, always move the ruler, not the fabric. Open up one fabric strip and check the spots where there were folds. If the fabric was not evenly lined up or the ruler was incorrectly positioned, there will be a bend at each of the folds in the fabric.

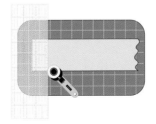

When cutting many strips, check after every three or four strips to make sure the strips are straight.

PIECING

For machine piecing, sew 12 stitches per inch, exactly 1/4" from the edge of the fabric, unless instructed to do otherwise in the pattern. To make accurate piecing easier, mark the throat plate with a piece of tape 1/4" away from the point where the needle pierces the fabric. Start and stop sewing at the cut edges, unless instructed to do otherwise in the pattern.

APPLIQUÉ

Appliqué pieces can be stitched by hand or machine. To hand appliqué, baste or pin the pieces to the background in stitching order. Turn the edges under with your needle as you appliqué the pieces in place. Do not turn under or stitch edges that will be overlapped by other pieces.

To machine appliqué, baste pieces in place close to the edges. Then stitch over the basting with a short, wide satin stitch using a piece of tear-away stabilizer under the background fabric. You can also turn the edges of appliqué pieces under as for needleturn appliqué, and stitch them in place with a blind-hem stitch.

PRESSING

Press each unit with a dry iron before progressing to the next step. Press all blocks, sashings, and borders before assembling the quilt top.

FINISHING YOUR QUILT
Marking Quilting Designs

Mark before basting the quilt top together with the batting and backing. Chalk pencils show well on dark fabrics, otherwise use a very hard

(#3 or #4) pencil or other marker for this purpose. Test your marker for removability first.

Transfer paper designs by placing fabric over the design and tracing. A light box may be necessary for darker fabrics. Precut plastic stencils that fit the area you wish to quilt may be placed on top of the quilt and traced. Use a ruler to mark straight, even grids. Masking tape can also be used to mark straight lines. Temporary quilting stencils can be made from clear adhesive-backed paper or freezer paper and reused many times. To avoid residue, do not leave tape or adhesive-backed paper on your quilt overnight.

Outline quilting does not require marking. Simply eyeball 1/4" from the seam or stitch "in the ditch" next to the seam. To prevent uneven stitching, try to avoid quilting through seam allowances wherever possible.

Basting

Tape the backing, wrong side up, on a flat surface to anchor it. Smooth the batting on top, followed by the quilt top, right side up. Baste the three layers together to form a quilt sandwich. Begin at the center and baste horizontally, then vertically. Add more lines of basting approximately every 6" until the entire top is secured.

Quilting

Quilting is done with a short, strong needle called a "between." The lower the number (size) of the needle, the larger it is. Begin with an 8 or 9 and progress to a 10 to 12. Use a thimble on the middle finger of the hand that pushes the needle. Begin quilting at the center of the quilt and work outward to keep the tension even and the quilting smooth.

Using an 18" length of quilting thread knotted at one end, insert the needle through the quilt top only and bring it up exactly where you will

begin. Pop the knot through the fabric to bury it. Push the needle straight down into the quilt with the thimbled finger of the upper hand and slightly depress the fabric in front of the needle with the thumb. Redirect the needle back to the top of the quilt using the middle or index finger of the lower hand.

Repeat with each stitch, using a rocking motion. Finish by knotting the thread close to the surface and popping the knot through the fabric to bury it. Remove basting when the quilting is complete.

If you wish to machine quilt, I recommend consulting one of the many fine books available on that subject.

Binding

Sew strips together with diagonal seams; trim and press seam allowances open.

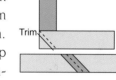

Fold the strip in half lengthwise, wrong side in, and press. Position the strip on the right side of the quilt top, aligning the raw edges of the binding with the edge of the quilt top. Leaving 6" of the binding strip free and beginning a few inches from one corner, sew the binding to the quilt with a 1/4" seam allowance measuring from the raw edge of the quilt top. When you reach a corner, stop sewing 1/4" from the edge of the quilt top and backstitch. Clip the threads and remove the quilt from the machine. Fold the binding up and away from the quilt, forming a 45° angle, as shown.

Keeping the angled fold secure, fold the binding back down. This fold should be even with the edge of the quilt top. Begin sewing at the fold.

Continue sewing around the quilt in this manner to within 6" of the starting point. To finish, fold both strips back along the edge of the quilt so that the folded edges meet about 3" from both lines of stitching and the binding lies flat on the quilt. Finger press to crease the folds. Measure the width of the folded binding. Cut the strips that distance beyond the folds. (In this case 1 1/4" beyond the folds.)

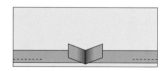

Open both strips and place the ends at right angles to each other, right sides together. Fold the bulk of the quilt out of your way. Join the strips with a diagonal seam, as shown.

Trim the seam allowance to 1/4" and press it open. Refold the strip, wrong side in. Place the binding flat against the quilt, and finish sewing it to the quilt. Trim excess batting and backing so that the binding edge will be filled with batting when you fold the binding to the back of the quilt. Blindstitch the binding to the back, covering the seamline.

Remove visible markings. Sign and date your quilt.

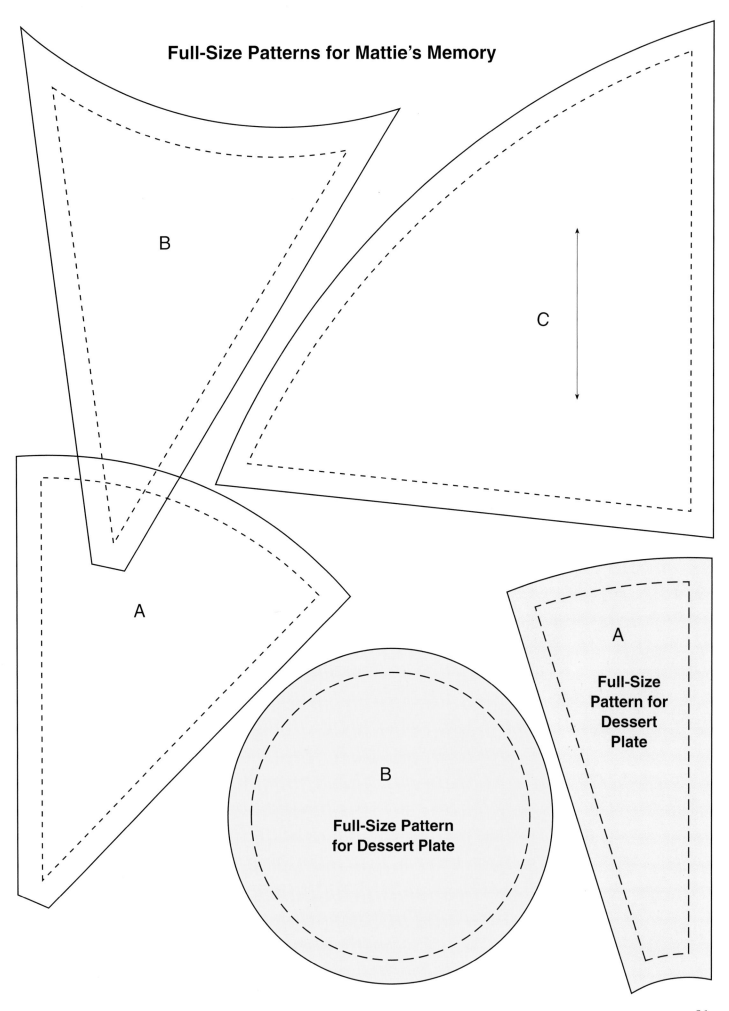

Full-Size Patterns for Mattie's Memory

B

C

A

A

Full-Size
Pattern for
Dessert
Plate

B

Full-Size Pattern
for Dessert Plate

31

Full-Size Patterns for Great-grandma's Sunbonnet Needlecase

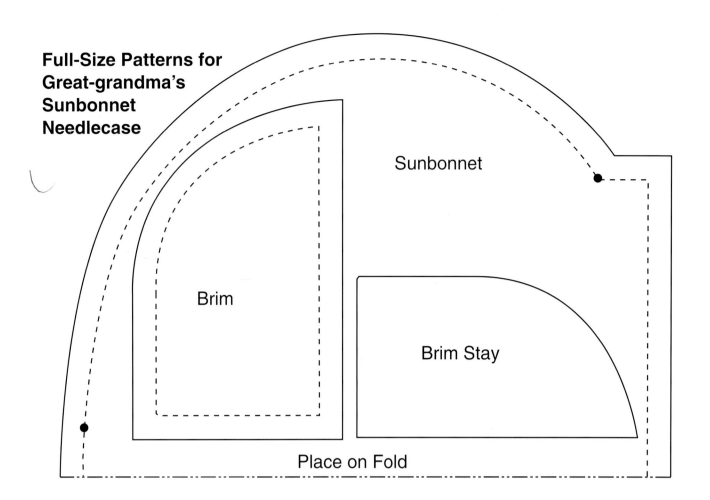

Sunbonnet

Brim

Brim Stay

Place on Fold

1973

1980

1990

1993

1997

In loving memory of my Grandpa

Harold Miller Squier

1909-1998

"Everything I needed to know, I learned by watching him. He was my Grandpa, teacher, role model, and most importantly, my friend."
—Diane Albeck-Grick